How to ...
Be a Kid

Chris Tait

Illustrated By Jim Paillot

Sterling Publishing Co., Inc.
New York

Edited by Jeanette Green
Designed by Renato Stanisic

**Library of Congress Cataloging-in-Publication Data
Available**

10 9 8 7 6 5 4 3 2 1

Published by Sterling Publishing Co., Inc.
387 Park Avenue South, New York, N.Y. 10016
© 2003 by Chris Tait
Distributed in Canada by Sterling Publishing
^{c}/o Canadian Manda Group, One Atlantic Avenue, Suite 105
Toronto, Ontario, Canada M6K 3E7
Distributed in Great Britain by Chris Lloyd
at Orca Book Services, Stanley House, Fleets Lane,
Poole BH15 3AJ, England
Distributed in Australia by Capricorn Link (Australia)
Pty. Ltd., P.O. Box 704, Windsor, NSW 2756 Australia
Printed in Hong Kong
All rights reserved

Sterling ISBN 0-8069-8503-8

Contents

Introduction

Kid is the name for a young goat. It's a stinky little thing that eats shoes and old cans. But don't let that bother you. You may be stinky, but that's not what this book is about.

There's another meaning for the word kid: "to deceive as a joke or to make fun of." That sounds a little better, doesn't it? And that must be why kids—that would be you—are called kids.

But is it really that easy?

Do you just show up in the world and know how make weird noises with your armpit? I don't think so! Are you born with perfect spitball style? No. It's an art, really. A science. And I'm going to let you in on the secrets.

Through my amazing 25-chapter methods, *How to Be a Kid* will teach you, young man or woman, just how to amaze, annoy, and amuse the world.

As you grow into your abilities, you will become a great kid and a world-class kidder. After all, it is more than your right. It is your duty to make root beer come pouring out the nose of your friends and family.

You'll learn how to blow spit bubbles, drop water balloons with precision, and whistle with two fingers just like old taxi drivers.

So, to you, young reader, I say good luck, bonne chance and wish you first-rate kidding for all your days.

—*Chris Tait*

How to ...
Increase Your Allowance

There's something controlling even about the word allowance. It is what you are "allowed." But you and I both know it should be called owe-lowance.

Of course, we can talk all we want, but the only way to really up the ante on your allowance is to enlist the help of your friends. That probably means sharing a chunk of your first raise. But after that, it's all gravy, kiddo!

To increase your allowance, you're going to need to stage a performance. Find a time when your parents are around. Now assemble your buddies.

Ask them to think up some great tall tales about the trouble they've gotten into because they had nothing to do. Parents for centuries have believed in a saying that goes something like this: "Idle hands are the Devil's playthings."

Trust me; your parents do not want you to have idle hands.

Your parents are not in the room, but you know they hear everything. So get your friends to tell you in a nice loud voice that they are grounded and have to go home early. Ask them (all-surprised-like): "What for?"

Now, it's their chance to shine. They have to tell stories that involve misplaced siblings, broken windows, dangerous construction sites, runaway cars, etc. As soon as they finish, kick them out.

Next, leave the room for about two minutes.

When you come back in, act downright droopy. Tell your parents that you were going to go out to buy comics or video games, but you don't have enough money. So, instead, you'll probably just go hang out by the corner where all that broken stuff is. You saw some neat razor wire and bricks...

Your parents will pull out their wallets and empty them on the table. I guarantee it.

How to ...
Tell a Ghost Story

What could be better than a good ghost story? Kids who can tell a ghost story that makes their friends scream, wet the bed, and develop nervous ticks are the pride of every camping trip and sleepover. These terrifying tales are best told in the dark or in unfamiliar surroundings, and you'll want a few special effects.

And the key to telling a great ghost story is VOLUME!

Now, this is not to suggest that you should sit around yelling out *The Legend of Sleepy Hollow* at your friends. If you do, you will very quickly find that you have none.

No. The trick is about the dynamic of volume. You should always start at a medium volume and grow gradually quieter and quieter.

By the middle of your story—the part where they go to look for what's in the basement or attic or to open the cupboard—you should be almost impossible to hear.

If you're doing this properly, your friends will be leaning in close to listen with their mouths wide open, and their soda-pops tipping and dripping all over their laps while they gaze sleepily into your eyes.

And that's when you want to whack them. Something like "And then, from around the dark corner, HE JUMPED OUT AND GRABBED THEM BY THEIR ANKLES!"

Take full advantage of this. It is your moment.

Try to make your eyes bug out of your head. Make your mouth open wider than the Grand Canyon. Let your tongue waggle. Yes, whippersnapper, I said waggle!

A good gauge to tell whether you're getting enough volume is to check for flying spit. Spit should be everywhere. There should be so much spit that you look like you have rabies.

And your friends? Your friends should be covered in soda, clinging onto each other for dear life, begging for their mommies. They might have to change their undies.

Two more elements make a truly great ghost story.

One: You need a flashlight. Be sure at all times to hold it so that it points up under your chin. This may permanently damage your vision, but the effect is worth it. The light will cast an eerie glow up your face that will make listeners shiver with fear.

Two: You should probably begin your ghost story by making the number of fools who venture into the cobwebs of a mysterious basement, attic, or graveyard in your story the exact number of people in your party. Do a quick head count. Name names if you have to.

Your story should begin something like: "It was a dark, dark night, and there were (quick count—one, two, three, four…) FIVE young travelers lost in the crypt…"

Go on, make 'em weep!

How to ...
Get Out of Doing the Dishes

Exactly how are you supposed to get into any kind of good trouble if you are up to your elbows in dishwater?

How can you set traps, lay ambushes, and generally create havoc when scrubbing soup pots? The very notion is ridiculous.

Dishes are for adults who think they are important and who clearly forgot how to have fun when dinosaurs were still roaming the earth.

As a true kid, just remember this saying: "Cleanliness is next to impossible!"

Perhaps the best defense against the "doing of the dishes" is to be terrible at doing them. This principle applies for almost all housework, really. (Even grown-up guys act like kids and pretend they don't know how to scour pans or sort laundry.)

Do the laundry just once with a nice new pair of red socks thrown in with the white towels and I guarantee it will be the last load you ever have to do. Of course, now you'll have pink gym shorts, but that will be worth it.

When it comes to the dishes, here's what you do. Find a pot full of something goopy and gross. Now, hold on there, Sport! Don't go washing that pot. Just dip it in the dishwater. Now, some of the goop will come out and that's acceptable, but you want to leave a good layer in there to get crusty. All right, that bit's done. Put it in the drying rack.

Now, find yourself some cutlery. Again, simply dip these in the sink as if you were flavoring them. Next up is the glassware. Now, mothers love glassware. Don't ask me why. If it's not spotless, something in their brains seizes and they freak.

Your best bet here is probably just to put a dot of dish soap in the bottom of each one and flip it into the dish rack. This will inevitably dribble down and dry out, leaving a nice film of soapiness. This is a particularly nasty taste with wine.

All of this will probably result in some back-and-forth helpful suggestions between you and your parental units. That's OK. Nod as if you are taking it all in and offer to do the dishes the next night.

Night two, repeat the above, just faster.

You will be written off as incapable of

learning even the most basic of household chores and will be sent out to play or into the other room. Everyone will shake his head and think you are a bit slow. But, deep down, you will know that you have won. And best of all, no prune hands!

Note: If this method fails, you may have to resort to the towel snap, which you'll find in an upcoming chapter. I'm here to help, after all.

Now listen: The homework excuse is a tradition as old as the cave people.

When you are coming up with an excuse for not having done your homework, you are stammering in the shadow of giants. Presidents, poets, and prosecutors have all had to fudge the homework excuse. The weight of history is upon you. So, step up, and have something brilliant in mind.

Simply claiming that the dog ate your homework is as bad as having done the actual work.

You might as well eat the pages yourself. No teacher worth his or her salt will take this "dog ate my..." stuff lying down. No, if you are going to avoid the homework, it is best to come up with something truly colossal.

In fact, to come up with a truly great homework excuse, you may have to spend more time thinking about the excuse than it would take to do the work. But this is entirely beside the point.

Think along these terms: Earthquakes. Tidal waves. Monsoons. Alien abductions. Your goal here is to confuse the teacher into saying something like: "All right, we'll deal with this later" or, better yet, "OK, well, bring it tomorrow."

And, as we all know, tomorrow is another day.

Below, you will find a few helpful starters that you may use until you get your homework excuse up to expert levels. And remember, even the good Doctor once had to do his homework, or, rather, to come up with an excuse for not doing it.

I COULDN'T DO MY HOMEWORK BECAUSE:

• All members of my family are devout pagans. Last night was the Feast of the Gilded Goat. That means no paper in the house. Goat's orders.

• I have an allergic reaction to night reading. I can only focus under natural light. Perhaps if I had this class off, I could go outside and work in the sun. Then I could get it done.

• I live in the part of town that was hit by that micro-monsoon last night. My entire street was flooded, and localized tropical hail hit my backyard. The lights went out, and we had to spend the night in the basement eating canned turnips by flashlight.

In these situations, it's also a good idea to make a face that's like the one you make after you eat a hot pepper by mistake. Choke back tears and try to make yourself a little flushed. In fact, now that I think about it, you might want to eat a hot pepper first.

In any case, these examples are really just prompts to get your brain working on something creative and exciting—your very own homework excuse! All this is infinitely more interesting than the homework itself, I can assure you.

How to ...
Fake Looking Sick

I can't even begin to capture the importance of this skill. This is really fundamental if you are going to have any fun at all. Some days, the idea of going to school is a lot like the idea of being crushed by a hippo. Too heavy to even contemplate!

Sometimes you just need to lie in bed or on your couch and watch cartoons or daytime television. But be forewarned: don't overact the fake.

You'll end up at the doctor's, and those guys are good at this stuff!

Your best bet is to get up a few minutes early and fill up a hot water bottle. Now, listen carefully for the adults in your house to wake up. They're bound to shuffle off to the bathroom. Now is your chance.

Put the hot water bottle on your forehead. This will feel slightly odd or slightly good, depending on your personality, but trust me.

Now, when you hear the creak of ancient knees coming your way, take your water bottle and shove it under the bed. Your parent will come in, take one look at your dismal face and go for the forehead. Which will be wonderfully hot.

Now, there will be some discussion about how you feel. I don't think I need to help you here. Saying you feel like watching bad television and eating ice cream and being waited on like the King of Siam is the wrong answer and you know it. You feel terrible.

Next they will produce the thermometer. They'll pop it under your tongue and ask you if you need anything. Why parents don't ask you before they pop it under your tongue is anyone's guess. But that's what they're like, aren't they? Of course, you need something, so send them off to get it. Now, back to the water bottle. Thermometer, meet boiling water.

Either lay your thermometer on the bottle snugly or, time permitting, pull the cap and hold it in the water for a while. This may result in spillage, but you can always claim that this is feverish sweat.

Again, be sure to do this so that your temperature is a bit up. A temperature of 168 is going to get you in the Emergency Room and stuck in the hospital hooked up to a machine for a week and written up in the record books. Similarly, mumps and measles take real practice to fake and anything to do with your stomach is going to get you medicated. My advice to you is to stick to the simple cold. Sniffle a bit and cough and stay in your pajamas all day.

And there you are; you are officially sick. Enjoy your day off, courtesy of the good Doctor. That's OK, you don't have to thank me.

How to ...
Launch a Spitball

Launching a spitball is a skill much like pulling a rabbit out of a hat. Of course, to pull a rabbit out of a hat, you need a rabbit and a hat. To launch a spitball, you just need spit, paper, and a straw or pen. The point, and there was one, was that they both work on the principle of distraction. Get your target to look away for an instant and you are all clear— to launch a spitball. (I can't help you with the rabbit bit.)

Spitballs are genius because they are so simple. Just rip up some everyday paper and roll them into little tiny balls. Now, put them in your mouth and soak them in good old-fashioned spit.

Next, find yourself a pen or a straw. You probably have a pen with the paper and the desk that you're sitting at. Useful things, these pens, once you take out the pen part, anyway. Just pop out the inside and voilà! You've got yourself a perfect little blowgun. Or try a jumbo drinking straw.

Now, you have two choices: The first is for your own amusement and the second will get the whole room going.

In option one, you attempt to make a pattern on the ceiling of your classroom. Simply put your pen up to your mouth, use your tongue to put the spitty ball of paper in the tube, lean your head back and let it rip. It should stick to the ceiling above you with a thwack and will dry into a paper pulp mess that will still be there when your grandchildren are launching their own spitballs in that same classroom.

The second, more fun, option is to spit one of your homemade slobber bombs at a friend.

Again, the spitball leads to more spitballs, but that's good. You'll have someone to spend detention with. And detention is a perfect place to hone option one.

When you're aiming at a friend, a good target is the hair. The only thing funnier than a spitball in the hair is one aimed at the neck. Hit your friends in the neck and they will bark like a dog and whack the spot like a mosquito bite before they figure out what's happened. This is sure to get the teacher on their backs, which is a kind of bonus fun that comes with the spitball.

As a final note on the spitball, you need to

watch the amount of spit applied. A really goopy spitball will simply slide out of the pen or straw and end up all over your desk. Worse yet, it may lodge in the chamber and leave you purple-faced and open for retaliation. That said, it's still easier than the hat trick, and you don't need to feed any rabbits.

How to ...
Blow Spit Bubbles

Well, seeing as how we're already talking about spit, we should broach the spit bubble. Blowing spit bubbles is a great time-passer. But it's not as easy as it looks.

First off, you have to get enough saliva in your kisser. Now, bring your tongue up to the roof of your mouth. As you slowly pull it away, release some air. This will form a delicate bubble.

Now, bring your tongue back up the roof of your mouth, behind it, to close the bubble. What you have is a perfect, fragile globe of saliva. How appetizing. But it gets better!

Now, what you need to do, with your tongue underneath your temperamental treasure, is to open your mouth and roll. Now, I know this chapter is called how to blow spit bubbles, but the truth is, if you blow on these suckers, they'll just pop. Spit is fun, but it's not very sturdy!

So, roll your spitball along your tongue until it's out in the open. When you get it out onto the tip of your tongue, just let it slide off. It should roll off and float away like a graceful little feather.

Of course, it won't do this the first couple of times. You're going to be doing a lot of drooling to get this right. But that's OK. A good time to practice creating spit bubbles is during a car trip or bus ride. You and a comrade can spend hours just slobbering and producing little bubbles.

When you finally get it right, it's best to try out your amazing new skill somewhere with height. The higher you are, the longer your spit bubble will fall. Think balconies here, like the kind you'll find in church.

You can watch your little bubbles sail down from the second tier and land lovingly on those fancy hats with a silent pop. Movie theater balconies, outdoor terraces, and decks above pool parties are also good for the spit bubble.

Again, make sure you're pretty good at this before giving it a shot in public. The last thing you need is to spit on some lady's head in church and have everyone see you doing it. You'll end up in confession forever and a day, and your parents will take it very personally. Never mind the innocent lady with the hat.

There will come a time in your life when you'll want to say to someone: "Why don't you take a picture? They last longer!"

You'll find yourself saying this because some other kid has decided to stare at you. The only people who should be staring at you need to know they'll have to beat you in a staring contest. Unless, of course, they're your family. Parents, sisters, and brothers probably already know exactly what kind of weird little person you really are.

The trick to winning a staring contest is simple, really. Don't stare. What I mean is don't glare and open your eyes as wide as they go and hope that you have the supernatural ability of not blinking. After all, this is not really a staring contest, is it? There is no judge for staring.

This is really a not-blinking contest and you can win that one by following these two simple steps.

Step One: Close your eyes tightly before the staring contest begins. Remember, we blink because our eyes dry out. So, keep your little eyeballs moist and juicy before you begin.

Step Two: Don't stare—squint! That's right. Squint. When the contest is on, your adversary will be glaring like a madman. But not you!

You will be exposing the least eyeball surface area. You will be relaxed and, what's more, mean-looking as all get out! You might even want to smile slightly, like you know something super cool.

Soon enough, your friend's eyeballs will be like the Sahara Desert. They will begin to dry up and sting. Even the tears will be sizzling away. But it's no use. You are a super cool, squinting, smirking staring-contest master.

Bring on the starers. You'll take them on at high noon, one at a time.

How to ...
Toast the Perfect Marshmallow

Oooooh, this is a tricky one. Anything to do with food is tricky. And you know, marshmallows are food. I know what you're thinking—no, they're not. They're delicious whipped chemical candy things that never, ever decompose. But that's not entirely true.

Marshmallows were originally made from the root of a plant called the marsh mallow that grew in, you guessed it, marshes! So, it's really a vegetable. Which makes it a great substitute for Brussels sprouts.

There are really two ways to cook a marshmallow. The first, more traditional app-roach, is called the Toaster.

The Toaster is that picture-perfect lightly golden brown work of art that makes everyone sitting around the campfire need a marsh-mallow. And, here's how you cook one: Rotate it over the fire on the end of a stick until it's toasted. Take it out. Very yummy and really, really boring.

No, my preference is for option number two: the Flaming Roaster. This baby has it all. Style, excitement, and a unique flavor. You pop it on your stick, hold it over the fire—and wait.

What you're after here is igniting sugar. Oh sure, your marshmallow will go through the Toaster phase, but that will soon pass.

Soon, a small fire will start on your marshmallow. Then, a great flame as the outside of your bonbon literally chars. Now it gets interesting.

You pull out your Flaming Roaster and give it a giant blow. It will smoke, which is good. Now you pull off the outer shell of caramelized sugar. Eat it. Crunchy, weird and, maybe, good.

What you have underneath is a whole new gooey mess. Take this, put it in the fire...and wait. You get the idea. Do this three or four times for each marshmallow. Four times the fun, double the flames, and some good smoke. Everyone will make fun of you, but wait and watch. Their next marshmallow will be a Flaming Roaster and not one of those pretty, stuck-up Toasters.

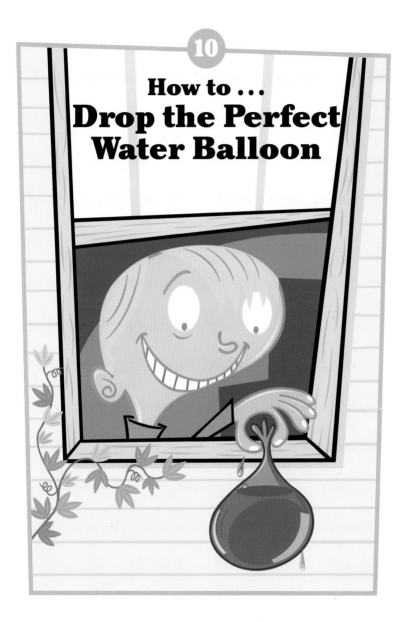

How to ...
Drop the Perfect Water Balloon

Water balloons are wonderful weapons of whimsy. Wow! Sorry, the "w" is stuck on my computer...

Dropping a water balloon, like so many other good wet gags, relies on surprise and an element of technical know-how. Overfill your water balloon in a moment of greed for the big sploosh, and you'll end up wearing it before you even get near the target!

Of course, water balloons should always be filled with the coldest water available. If you can get it straight from a glacier, go for it! Water-balloon dropping is all about that one second of freezing shock when your victim gasps with sudden surprise.

If you miscalculate even a little, then what you'll have is the remnants of a balloon lying behind someone whose ankles are a little damp. What a letdown!

So, the trick with dropping the perfect water balloon is about balance. Very Zen. Just full enough to be a doozy and cold enough to deliver a wallop.

The second element involves finding a good place to drop your balloon and laying the bait.

Also, you should find a place to hide with your treasure that is not going to see you squished if you fall. Standing on the roof looks like a good idea, but when you slip, pitch onto the sidewalk, and end up like road pizza with bits of balloon in it, you're not going to think so.

Instead, find yourself an open window that overlooks your door and lie in wait. Again, you're going to need a story to get this thing off the ground.

Some good examples of this are...

"Hey Sis, there's someone at the door for you!"

"Uncle Ted, I'm outside. Can you come help me fix my bike?"

Once you get these monkeys under your scope, let 'er rip! But remember, it's all about timing. Miss and you just look immature. A direct hit, however, showcases you as a juvenile delinquent with style and a real future.

On a final note, making one water balloon always leads to another, but after a certain point balloons turn into buckets and finally, the battle for control of the hose. So you may want to start off wearing your slicker and galoshes!

How to ...
Sneak a Peek
at Christmas
Presents

Wow! This is a hot potato. Here you enter some really touchy terrain that could spell bad luck. Or lumps of coal next year!

That said, you are not an adult, and snoop you will. Privacy is something you'll care about and defend when you're a teenager. For now, it's just an abstract concept.

So, you've made the moral decision to "sneak the peek." Who can it hurt? It'll be your stuff sooner or later, you think, trying to make yourself feel better. You know that Santa knows who is naughty or nice, but you figure, hey, this year's counting is done. By now, St. Nick is onto next year, and I'll have a whole year to make up for what I'm about to do.

Plus, I really need to know if I'm going to get that new video game console, or I'm going to die!

Who am I to argue? After all, I'm only here to help. So, here's what to do. First of all, find a time to look when you know everyone will be out for more than ten minutes.

I can't count the number of kids who think they'll have enough time to crawl into their parents' closets while their moms are brushing their teeth. Nope, what you need is a nice hour and a map! Why a map? Because you're going to go barging in there, move everything in the closet, attic, or basement, find your beloved game, toy, or other treasure, and forget about everything else. Half an hour later, you'll look up and realize that you have no idea where everything originally was. Then, you are as cooked as the Christmas dinner, turkey!

So, when you go to said hiding place, take a moment and block it out. Figure out how everything is lying and then—Go for it! Root like the truffle pig that you are. But I must warn you: You've opened a can of worms, and they may very well be your wriggling worms.

Come Christmas morning, you have to pretend to be incredibly excited by something that you've already seen. Something you've already played with. Something you're already bored with. Not fun.

And here's a final caution. Think about this. You look, and it's not there…

Now what?

How to ...
Make Weird Noises from Your Armpit

Not to put too fine a point on it, but some things are funny because they are gross. Making your armpit noises falls under this category. Dumb and vulgar and very, very funny.

Now, no doubt, there will be some girls and guys who will be offended by this type of behavior. Some kids will think that only buffoons make noises from their armpits. Don't worry about them. I'll show you how to get them later in this chapter.

For now, let's start with the actual mechanics of the armpit noise. To begin, it's essential that you are wearing something on your torso that you can get under. You can't make armpit noise in a snowsuit. I'm the first to admit that this is a real shame. But we are brave and we carry on.

To make the armpit noise, slide your hand in a cupped position up under your shirt. You're going to want to shower first. You don't want B.O. hands all day, do you? Cup your armpit. Now quickly bring your arm down. This should create a bellows that shoots air out towards your back.

At first, the wind will just gust out. After a few tries, however, you will hear something like a small, surprised duck. Soon, as you increase the speed and suction, you will hear a sound like a balloon popping. Keep practicing.

At some point, you should hear a sound that makes you cringe. Now you are getting

somewhere.

This in itself should amuse the heck out of you. But let's get back to the nay-sayers and the snobs. This is where you learn to throw the noise of your armpit. Stand behind them or just beside them, and when no one is looking, slide your hand up under your shirt.

Now, very quickly, do your worst. Your most horrible armpit artillery. Whip your hand back out and step away, in disgust, from your enemy. Cringe and look accusingly. You may even want to fake retching and stagger away, depending on how dramatic you are feeling.

They will protest, but who will believe them? They will be shunned and reviled, if only for the afternoon. Serves them right, those Goody Two-shoes. Ah, it's good to be a kid, ain't it? And better to be one who has mastered the ninja art of the armpit noise.

Going to sleep is something kids are made to do by old people. You're not tired! But this argument won't get you very far.

Really, you have two choices. Option one is all about preparedness and planning. I call this one BEDROOM CENTRAL. The logic behind this is simple. Your parents don't want you to go to sleep. They want you to go to your room and leave them alone so that they can have the TV to themselves.

So, all you have to do is to get out of their hair. They'll want your lights off, so you're going to need a flashlight. And some comic books. These you can just store under your bed. And, as long as you're going to be up all night, you might as well have all the comforts of home, so you should stock up on food.

Do this slowly over a couple days. Some chips maybe. Cookies fit in sock drawers and won't go stale for days. You can even fit a can of soda-pop into one of your rolled-up pairs of socks. And with that, you can curl up, covers over your head, with hours of flashlight time, comics, and junk food.

Option two is called the PILLOW

PRETENDER. This will require more preparation, but is totally worth it. First off, in the days before your all-nighter, find some old pillows around the house and begin stashing them in your room. If you can't find any, you can use pillowcases stuffed with sweaters.

The idea here is to find and build a replacement body for yourself that can double for you in your bed while you're not in it. Simply place these pillows in your bed under the covers in the same sort of shape that you take up when you sleep. Turn off the lights and observe your handiwork. In the dark, it's going to pretty much work.

Wait till everyone's in bed. Now, it's all about finding a way into the family room undetected. Once there, the place is yours for comic books, video games with the sound off, or very, very quiet TV. Again, if you get caught, you're on your own. Hey, I don't want to be grounded.

14

How to ...
Control Your Dreams

If you're reading this chapter, I'm going to assume one of two things. One, you are being made to go to sleep, and there's just no way out of it. Two, you have been caught stuffing pillows with sweaters, and you're under house arrest.

Whatever the scenario, this is a great skill to have. There's nothing worse than having to go to sleep and finding out that you're simply dreaming about school. You'll just end up in one of those stupid dreams where you're in class wearing just your underwear and trying to write a test with a fish for a pen. Trust me; that's the pickled eggs talking.

No, what you want to do is to have dreams where you can fly. Dreams where you are the King of the Sea. Dreams where you never strike out and never, ever forget to wear pants.

The trick to this is to simply prepare your brain. Think of it as sleep studying. It's not as bad as it sounds. All you have to do is figure out what it is you want to dream about.

If you want to be in King Arthur's court, spend a couple of minutes before you sleep reading about the king's life and times. Pictures also help. Look into the world you want to be part of and absorb it.

Now, lie back in your bed and close your eyes. Try to see the round table or the Lady of the Lake. Imagine what her voice would sound like. Think about the smells. Soon enough, you'll be there, drifting off, and having adventures that will make the wasted time of sleeping suddenly worthwhile.

You'll be excited to go to bed, just so that you can get back to the story. It also helps to keep a journal by the bed so that in the morning you can record what happened the night before. That way, you can teach yourself to pick up where you left off.

Of course, with your luck, you'll end up in a duel or a joust, and you'll pull a fish out of your scabbard and realize you're not wearing any pants. But that's just your brain making fun of all your hard work. Pay it no mind.

1

15

How to ...
Make Bread-Twist
Finger Flickers

By now, you are well aware that you can have fun with just about any household object. One of the best of these is the Bread-Twist Finger Flicker. It combines the coolest parts of a Frisbee with the advantage of being able to keep it in your pocket. And each and every loaf of bread has two of these for you to have fun with. It's perfect, really.

So, what is this wonderful flicker you say, and how do I make it work for me? Take a look at the loaf of bread in your kitchen. At the very end of it, where it's twisted shut, is a small plastic clip. It probably has the date on it when the bread starts turning into penicillin. If this date is several weeks ago, stop making sandwiches.

Steal this little clip from the loaf of bread. Tie the bag so that no one will mind. It's really not that vital a piece of equipment. Take the little clip and snap it in half down the middle so that you end up with two sort of comma-looking shapes. Each one can become its own flying flicker! Now, here comes the part that's a little fiddly. Here's what you need to do: Set up one of these flickers on your middle finger, just under the nail, so that the thicker end is facing toward your palm.

Next, it's just a simple flick. Put your thumb over the middle finger, cock it back, and let 'er rip! What you'll see is that these things fly forever and really move. And, you've got two of them. Which means you and your pal can practice shooting for distance or line up action figures or dolls along the back of the couch and take target shots at them.

The only problem with this innovation is that you're bound to loose them in the toaster, behind the baseboard, or in the lawn. And by then, you will be addicted.

You'll be de-clipping bread at your friend's houses and walking through the grocery store or convenience store aisles and looking at row after row of them. They're just sitting there waiting for you. You have to have them. Imagine having a million of them all for your own.

Stop right there. The last thing I need is to go to the grocery store, pick out a loaf of bread, and have it fall all over the floor so that you can play bread-twist finger flicker! Sometimes I wonder why I even tell you how to do these things…

16

How to ...
Blow a Bubble

But everyone can blow bubbles, I hear you say. Wrong you are, chap. Bubble blowing is harder than long division. Too big and you're covered in a face full of gum, too small and you are a laughing stock.

That said, bubble blowing is not, as some of my colleagues have suggested, a natural-born talent. You do not simply emerge a bubble-blowing genius. It's all about practice. Oh, and good gum.

If you're going to start off with that bad, chalky, baseball card gum, just skip this chapter. It'll never work. And you'll never really have enough gum to practice with. Ten or eleven chews, and that stuff is like chomping on a ball of yarn. Yuck!

Now, take your good gum of choice (flavor is irrelevant although grape is pretty darn good), and chew it up until it's good and supple.

Move it with your tongue to between your front upper teeth and your front lower teeth. These probably have real toothy names, but, hey, I'm not a dentist.

Now, chomping with just these four teeth,

roll the gum into a tube and begin to poke at it with your tongue. What you're doing here is creating a pocket for you to blow air into when you're good and ready.

By now, the gum should be spread fairly evenly over your teeth like a parachute, waiting for the wind. Well, I guess it's really kites that wait for the wind, but you know what I mean.

And now, it's time to blow. I should warn you that what will happen is that your bubble will burst. But that's all right. That's what all bubbles do. They are built to burst. The talent comes in getting them to a sizable bubble and getting them to pop like firecrackers in a way that will amuse you or your pals.

And that, dear reader, takes practice. But that's why gum comes in packs. So you can practice until your jaw hurts.

Soon, you'll be the kid who blows the bubble too big and it pops and ends up not only hanging from his nose but in his hair.

I know, you can hardly wait.

The Ultimate Bubble Chart

Laughing Stock   **1/2-inch round**
Of use only for beginners. Get more air into
that sucker.

The Player   **1-inch round**
Good for walking with bubble fully inflated,
strutting your stuff. Unimpressive to the true
professional.

Da Bomb   **2-inch round**
The consummate bubble. Stretched to capacity,
almost as thin as air, fully obscures nose and
chin. Impressive.

The Firecracker   **3-inch round**
If you have blown this bubble, you have blown
this bubble. By now, you have hair full of gum
and sticky eyebrows. Ick!

17

How to ...
Make Your
Babysitter Crazy

To begin with, ask yourself why you have a babysitter. Are you a baby? I don't think so. Do you need to be watched like a hawk to keep you out of trouble? Well, all right, that one's a bad example. But really, shouldn't you just be allowed to have the run of the house? It's your house, isn't it?

So, you have a babysitter, and there's not much you can do about it. What you can do is to drive the babysitter batty. After all, the babysitter is there for your amusement.

You can start this process by taking advantage of your house. This only works with new babysitters, but essentially the trick is simply to hide. You know your house. Find that one great spot that you used to use as a fort, stock up on comics, and disappear.

Soon enough, your babysitters will be beside themselves. They'll be tearing the house apart, thinking the worst. They'll think that you've been abducted by aliens or that you've run away for good.

Don't stay there for too long or else they'll call the police—or worse, your parents. About ten or fifteen minutes of hiding should be enough to make the poor teenager bonkers. Then simply walk by the sitter as she's looking behind the couch and under the carpet. Saunter into the kitchen, get a glass of milk, and walk back out. Your teenage sitter will stand there, all sweaty, mouth gaping open like a mailbox. Savor the sweet taste of victory.

Next up is the crank call. Get yourself to the phone. Call one of your pals. Tell him to call you but that as soon as you pick up, he should hang up the phone. Get him to do this, oh, thirty or forty times. On the forty-first time he calls, tell him to ask for you. When the sitter answers the phone, he will practically scream hello. This is when your friend asks for you, very calmly. Pick up the phone, talk to your friend for a few minutes and, as you do, start looking at the sitter as if she should be in a cuckoo clock.

Finally, you can have some fun with food. If your sitter feeds you anything prepared at all—soda-pop, a cookie, whatever, wait for about five minutes and start looking a little odd. Ask her very politely if what you've just eaten had any sugar or preservatives in it. Of course, it does. Now look very concerned. Tell her that you are allergic to preservatives.

When she asks what symptoms she should be looking for, tell her that you usually turn blue, your lips swell up like dune buggy tires, and you often faint. Now go lie down on the couch and watch television. The sitter will freak out and wait on you hand and foot while you lounge. And, of course, stop this game short of her having to call your parents or the doctor. The only thing worse than getting caught is being found out by a guy who can give you a shot with a long needle. When you get bored with this game, tell her you feel OK. Then go off to concoct some other devious plan. As always, this is simply a starter kit for other schemes. Enjoy!

18

How to . . .
Avoid the Shower

As a final note on being a kid, I would like to point out that if you are not at least semi-dirty at all times, you're really not trying hard enough. Anyone can act mischievous, but you just need to look under his or her sparkling fingernails to know that kid's really a poseur. Real kids are filthy from fun and proud of it.

In fact, the whole myth about cleanliness is one of control. Adults want you to be clean and scrubbed so that your spirit is literally dampened. Why is it important to clean behind your ears? So that you are trained to routinely clean behind your ears. It's a vicious cycle.

What you need to do is to avoid, at all costs, being too clean. Now, I don't mean that you should let yourself go so far that people are crossing the street to avoid the smell of you. That wouldn't be any fun, now would it? But by and large, one bath a week is tons. After all, the once-a-week bath was the stuff of frontier days. (Well, they also had outhouses, but never mind.) These clean freaks who want you soaked daily are out of their minds!

One hour of bath or shower, shining, polishing, cleansing time is one less hour of fun and frivolity. So, we're agreed that this excessive bathing will do you no good. Now, how do you avoid it?

Begin with the hair damper. Again, comics are a great help here. Stash some comics under the sink. When you're told to go take a bath, just go upstairs, get good and comfy on the throne, and settle in for some good reading.

After about twenty minutes of this, just hop up, re-stash your comics, and run the tap for a few seconds. When you get the temperature you want, just run your hands underneath and slide them through your hair. Voilà! You are freshly showered. Listen, if it was good enough for the pioneers, it's good enough for you.

However, this will really only work for a little while. Eventually, your parents are going to march you in there and expect to see you coming out smelling like roses. This is where you delve into your father's toiletries. Never forget that the sense of smell is one of the most powerful senses we possess. In fact, many perfumes and powders were created for people just like you who avoided this odd bathing ritual.

So, after a good half hour of messing around, just pop open some scented junk in the medicine chest and plonk it behind your ears. If it is deodorant, swipe the stuff under your arms and away you go. Perfume should just be strategically applied. Too much and you'll smell like your Aunt Ethel. And that's never a good thing.

At some point, you will have to cave in and have a bath. And this can be OK. Just make sure it's on your own terms and that they let you practice your front crawl stroke. Remember, dirt reveals character, and your character is to be a kid.

How to ...
Whistle with Two Fingers

Oh, this one is superfly! Anyone who can whistle with his fingers should be given the keys to the city and a lifetime supply of pizza!

These whistles are the loudest ever and make you look both tough and lazy. Like you could call out using your voice, but you are sooo over that. Plus, there's that great noise—"whee, oh, whee!" You just know everyone is going to drop a spoon and stand at attention.

So, what's the trick? Why is this whistle so loud and so fun? As the safe cracker says, it's all in the fingers.

When you do a taxi whistle (which is what these babies are called) you're really opening and stretching your lips into an elastic surface for air to pass through.

Think of the opening of a balloon. When you want it to make that squealing noise that we all know and love, you have to pull it taut so that you force air through a small, tight opening.

Well, your fingers are doing the same thing. Once you get those digits into your mouth on either side of your teeth, you just need to pull out a little.

Next, it's on to the tongue. Curl it back toward your tonsils and push it up against the roof of your mouth. Now, try to tighten your lips into a regular whistle shape and blow.

The result will be the loudest thing heard for miles. People should drop bottles, snap their pencils in half, and generally go nuts. But you'll get their attention all right. Do this in school, and you'll get their detention. But that's another matter.

Oh, also worth noting is the finger choice.

Option One: Use either the index (pointer) finger of one hand and the pinky of the same hand.

Option Two: Use both pinkies and requires you to bring both hands up to your mouth.

My personal choice is option two because I think you look more impressive with both hands in your mouth. And I don't mean just anybody. I mean you. Now go wash your hands.

20

How to . . . Cannonball into a Pool

Ah, the cannonball! That perfect corruption of a dive in which you make yourself into a projectile and sacrifice all dignity just to get a laugh.

When you get older, you will realize that life is like a cannonball.

But for now, you must simply do the cannonball. Over and over. The object of the cannonball is to displace all the water into the pool onto the dry towels of loved ones. Do not stop until this happens.

Cannonballs are not really about form. It doesn't matter how you look doing a cannonball. Everyone looks stupid doing one, and that is part of the fun. The real art is in the splash.

Of course, you have to be a good swimmer, and you need water deep enough so that you don't get hurt and hit bottom too quickly. Also, no other kids should be swimming nearby. If you collide, you could cause a serious accident. So think of big, relatively deep ends and go for it!

To begin with, you must try to make the biggest splash. This is quite easily done.

Simply run (safely) and jump up into the air over water. Now, pull up your legs to your chest and wrap your arms around your legs. Tuck the whole thing in and try to land butt first.

You will make a big splash. Good. You have now completed phase one. Phase two is to make the highest splash.

This is all about making your body into as tight a ball as possible. The tighter your body is tucked, the more like a ball you are, the more the water will go straight up.

For this, you will need a judge. This will lead to fighting, which will lead to phase three.

Phase three is the Intentionally Directed Cannonball Splash. Again, have no fear of this technical name.

The point here is that, with a little angling of your by-now-perfect cannonball, you can actually choose who, on deck or rock, to soak. Pick your target, angle your body and voilà! You have become the smart cannonball.

This should amuse you all year-round or at least until the water freezes.

21

How to ...
Win a Thumb War

Now it occurs to me that there may be those among you, dear readers, who have never engaged in thumb warfare. There may be some who are thumb pacifists. To you, I say congratulations. Skip this chapter and go smell a rose or pet a bunny.

For the rest of us, it's a war zone out there, and our little opposable digits are all we have.

Thumb wars are right up there with spitballs as great time wasters and detention-getters. But they're also a great way to win admirers and make your friends look like dunces.

For those of you who are new to combat, a thumb war is a game in which you wrap your four fingers in an almost fist through your friend's same hand. For example, left to left. What should be left are two vicious thumbs and the battlefield for your upper hands.

You start the game by crossing thumbs eight times while you both say: "One, two, three, four. I declare a thumb war."

Then, you wrestle thumbs and try to pin your pal's thumb and count to three. Sounds easy? Believe you me, it's tricky, and some of those greasy thumbs are sneaky.

First off, I want to tell you about a way to win that's above board. It's simple but effective. What you need to do is to mimic a technique perfected by a boxer named Mohammed Ali. You just keep dancing. Bob and weave.

Don't even go for the other thumb. Let him do all the work trying to pin you down. Trust me, it's much harder to pin a thumb than it is to make one move back and forth. The trick here? Agility and endurance.

Wear down that thumb. Make him sweat it a little. Then, when he looks over and out, you lunge in there and clobber him. Pin him down; show no mercy. Ah, war is heck.

The second way to win is to cheat. But only a little... Just jump the gun by a millisecond. You count out the chant: "One, two, three, four. I declare a thumb war!" By the time you get to war, you're on top of that thumb.

Squish him flat, count to three very quickly, and pull your hand away.

This will also give you something to argue about, which is half the point. But if they tell you that you jumped the gun and cheated, well then, I never told you to do it. I don't know what you're talking about.

How to . . .
Make a Thumb Puppet

So there you are with five minutes to kill and nothing to amuse you but a marker or a ball point pen. But you have nothing to write on. Are you kidding? Look no further than yourself. You are your own canvas. You are a blank page waiting to be covered in graffiti!

Soon enough, you will learn to make the illustrious thumb puppet. After all, if you're going to draw on yourself, you might as well make a face, develop a ridiculous accent for that voice, and start mocking other people. Right?

Thumb puppets are as easy or as complex as you want them to be. For the most basic thumb puppet, simply start with the hand opposite to your writing hand. This is simply because it's going to be a lot easier to draw with the right hand, right? Hand. Sorry, I got lost there. (Or the left, if you're a lefty. Didn't mean for you to be left out.)

Now, with the hand that will be your puppet, make a fist. Take this fist and slide your thumb up a little so that it covers the second knuckle of your index finger. Now, using that knuckle as a pivot, wiggle the thumb up and down a little. This is the bottom jaw of your puppet face. Can you see it?

This obviously means that the knuckle closest to your hand will be the middle of the forehead. On either side of this, draw a pair of eyes. Add a little nose and fill in the lips and you're done. You have a proto-puppet.

But that's just the beginning. Now, if you have the tools available, why not add some lipstick? There must be some lying around somewhere. Better yet, add some glasses and some facial hair. Heck, do all three!

As you're beginning to see, this puppet could be anyone.

So, why stop at just making a puppet? Why not make a caricature? This is when you make someone's face that you know and make it say ridiculous things.

Now, this is getting to be fun.

Develop a voice to go along with your handy puppet. Try something bizarre and theatrical. Now, just by working that thumb up and down, you have a talking show that will amuse your friends for hours. But wait, a one-puppet show? Why not gang up?

Get your friends to make a puppet on their hands, too! This will also make it easier to explain to the teacher that you haven't gone mad. Now, your puppets can talk, interact, and, with the simple addition of a pencil in each puppet's mouth, they can duel to the death! Suddenly, you are your own touring theatrical troupe, and you can apply for government funding. Did you really think you had nothing to do!

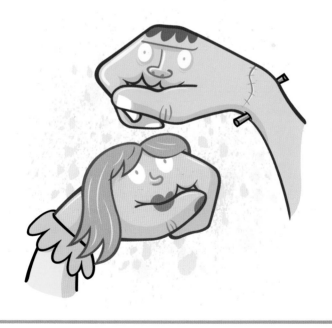

How to ...
Snap a Towel

You know, I don't even know if I should be telling you how to do this. Sure, it's fun. But if you give somebody a good welt, they're going to come looking for me! So, I guess my best advice here is not to get too good at snapping.

As always, remember that one good towel snap deserves another, and you'll get yours when it comes time. All right, enough with the warnings. On to the snappage!

This skill is a great way to get out of doing the dishes. You will become so annoying that no one will want you around! But more than that, the towel snap is a talent to torture your brothers and sisters with.

To snap a towel, begin with a smallish one. A dish towel, for instance. You can always work your way up to the mammoth beach towel. Start small, young grasshopper, and you will become a master.

Now, to practice, you'd best be alone. If you warm up in front of people, they'll be expecting it. Then half the charm is gone. Find yourself something to snap against, like a wall or some cupboards.

Hold a small handful of the towel in your hand in a loose fist. Let the rest hang towards the ground. Next, begin slowly spinning your hand clockwise. You will see that towel is now beginning to assume a shape like a twister. There is a circular shape in the middle and the bottom is curving out like a bellbottom. This is good. You are almost ready to snap.

To snap, simply move from your circling spinning and flick your wrist quickly towards your target's butt or legs. The spin will naturally continue and the towel will whip up like, well, like a whip!

The first couple of times you do this, your towel will probably just flop against the wall. Don't give up. Keep spinning and snapping, and within a few minutes, you will land one. Suddenly, your towel will touch the cupboard, and you will hear something like a cap going off. Suh-NAP! It just sounds great.

Now, you understand what you must do. You will begin looking for someone to snap. But remember, I'm telling you, if you have older siblings, they will have been doing this for years and will be better at it than you. So watch out. It's best to pick on kids your own size. And one final note—the only thing worse than a towel snap is a wet towel snap. Your days at the beach will never be the same!

How to ...
Fake Hawking a Loogie

This chapter is not for the faint of heart. Those of you easily grossed out, skip ahead.

We are about to venture, my prettys, into the land of...THE LOOGIE. Now, what in Great Gopher's name, you may be asking, is a loogie? A loogie is not quite spit and not quite snot. It is in the nether region between. It is the snotty spit. Spit with weight. I know, icky.

When you see someone hawk (or spit) a loogie, everyone cringes. It's gross, it's vile, but wait, what if you could make people think you were spitting a loogie into their hair from behind without really doing it? Ah ha! Now you're interested, aren't you? You might even know someone who needs this done to him. You're not a very nice person, are you?

To begin this essential talent, you must close your eyes and listen. Focus. Think of all the times you've heard someone hawk a loogie.

I know, I know, get over it!

Now, try to make that noise with your mouth. First, draw in air deeply through your nose. Now, make a noise like you are bringing something up from your throat. Next, pretend to spit.

Try this a few times until it's convincing. Now you're getting it. Now, pick a victim. The added trick here is a good strong gust of air. From behind, your loogie will sound convincing enough. But if you step right up behind someone and, at the end of your loogying, blow hard enough to part his hair, he'll freak out!

Next, your victim will drop everything he is doing and bring his hand up to his hair to check, as if you really hawked a loogie in his hair. Now, he will be confused and terrified. He will turn around and look at you with big googly eyes and I guarantee he will say only one thing: "What did you just do?"

And, of course, you are duty-bound to answer: "What are you talking about?"

Just try and do it with a straight face, will you?

How to ...
Make a Sound Like Dripping Water

doink

This one used to be called water torture, but those days are over. You're just as likely to hear it called "doink" these days, and that's what it really sounds like. This type of naming is onomatopoeia. That's a fancy word for naming something after what it sounds like. And what it sounds like is dripping water. Does this make any sense to you?

Now, why would you want to do this? Because you can. Some day, you'll be in some class where they are teaching you fancy words for naming things after what they sound like, and you'll look out the window and sigh.

But if you exhale and bring your tongue up to the roof of your mouth at the same time, a sort of whistling sound will come out. Do this a couple times and you can make this sound end in a sort of drip sound. Now, try it again without exhaling. Just use your tongue to force the noise out and end it with the drippy slap of your tongue hitting the roof of your mouth.

OK, now you're ready for part two. By now, other students will be looking, but that's all right. What's about to happen next will unify you in stupidity and you will be on the same page.

Take your middle finger and put it in the flicking position wrapped under your thumb. Now, bring it up to your cheek. Just as you are making the noise you know how to make, flick your cheek.

The effect, done properly, will sound like a drip in a cave. Done really well, it will sound like a drop of water from an icicle over a cave with a huge echo. This all depends on how big your mouth is and how good you get at this. But to get really good, you have to keep doing it. Do it once and every kid in class will start doing it because it's so cool.

And really, you need them as cover. Because the teacher is going to turn around and glare at you. Look around innocently. Now, if the rest of the class starts doing it after she turns her back, you cannot be blamed.

The trouble with this is, really, that to get it to championship levels, you have to flick your cheek a million times and you will end up with two red cheeks and an aching head. But just try to stop once you get it. I dare you. You are now a fully addicted Doinker. Your parents will be so proud.

Conclusion

Well, that's it for now. I hope I've helped you realize your full potential and that you now know how to cause havoc wherever you lay your hat.

With these methods under your belt, you are now a fully sanctioned, card-carrying kid. You are licensed to practice in any state and should feel free to unleash mayhem (well, a little chaos anyway).

As a final note, I'd just like to say that time is ticking. Get out there. One day you will look back and wonder why you didn't if you don't act now.

I know you will make the armpit trumpet, the water-balloon drop, and the loogie loft until the sun goes down. I'm counting on you. One day you, too, may have to pass your hard-earned wisdom on to another generation of kids. Until then, happy kidding!

—Chris Tait, Grown-Up Kid

About the Author

Chris Tait is the author of several children's books, including *Ridiculous Tongue-Twisters, Ridiculous Knocks-Knocks,* and *Ridiculous Riddles,* all available from Sterling Publishing Co., Inc.. His other books are ridiculous, too. They just don't say so in the title. Chris writes from Toronto, Canada, where he lives with his wife, Kim, and his son, Franklyn, whom Chris has been teaching to be a kid. Both are silly but not quite ridiculous. They share their house with a very serious cat named Kitchou. When he's not dreaming up new books, Chris composes music.

Index